Master Mind Reader

Scott Xavier presents

Tricky

Business

Proven Mind Tricks for Corporate Sales

Chenow Publishing 2008

Plainfield, IL.

Cover design & illustrations digitally created
by Xavier Designs

Copyrighted 2008 by Scott Xavier All Rights Reserved.

No part of this book may be reproduced, in whole or in part, without the specific written permission of the author. Unless otherwise stated, all material is copyrighted by Scott Xavier and Chenow Publishing.

First Edition

Ahoy, Fight piracy...

Printed, written, designed, and powered in the United States of America.

Edited by Scott Chenow, Walter King Jr, & Bernice Kalouris

-Chenow Publishing-
Plainfield, Illinois

ISBN: 978-0-6152-0938-8
Library of Congress Control Number: 2008904392

www.ScottXavier.com

.:For those who have helped me craft the magic. Without whom this would have never come to realization:.

--My father, Jori, Bernice, Greg Baas, Paul Haley, Christopher Carter, Walter King Jr., and all of my family & friends!

-TABLE OF CONTENTS-

IN THE BEGINNING… 10

THE ONLY ONE WHO WILL MAKE YOU A SUCCESS IS YOU! 11

the **ATTACK PLAN** 13

WHODOO VOODOO? 17

the **Words of Wisdom** 19

HE GUT YOU WON'T WANT TO LOSE… 21

Elementary, my Dear Watson… 25

Stress, What is it Good for? 27

MIND READING 29

the **Effect:** 32

NLP Thought Detection 33

the **Psychic Detective** 36

the **Cold Read** 38

ULTRA MEMORY 40

the **Secret of Memory** 41

Memorizing Names 44

Memorizing Numbers 44

MIND CONTROL 47

    Rule of Attraction 50

    Phone 101 51

    Time is a Precious Commodity: 52

    Eye Contact & Personal Space 52

    Be Where the Clients Are 52

    Win ANY Argument 53

Suggestion and Persuasive Language 54

Hypnosis History: 57

The Xavier Self Hypnosis Method 64

    Communication & Seduction 75

    Claustrophobia 77

    Lose Weight 78

    The Overview of the Xavier Induction of Positive Growth 79

Advanced Thought Influence Concepts 79

    Bait your enemies 80

    Actions speak louder 81

    WAR what is it good for 81

    Keep them hooked 81

    Become their friends 81

    Complete destruction 82

    Calculated insanity 82

    King Kong ain't got nothing 82

    Concentrate your forces 82

    Re-create yourself 83

    Cleanliness is next to 83

    Best laid plans 83

Oddball 83
Become royalty 83
Focus never get lost 83
Work on their hearts 84
Reflections 84

SCOTT XAVIER **AT A GLANCE**... **86**

In the Beginning…

My name is Scott Xavier and I am a mind reader. When I was eight years old I developed diabetes. My doctor at that time told me I could do anything with my life. Being a smug and smart ass kid, I told him I wanted to bend spoons using my mind like the guy on TV. Since that day, I have been back engineering the paranormal and crafting moment of mystery in my audience's lives.

I have developed many techniques for getting inside the minds of others, and at some point I realized how these techniques could advance business. This is what you have in your hand right now. Welcome to Tricky Business…

--Dr. Scott Xavier, D.D.
Motivational Mind Reader – Mentalist - Psychic Entertainer

"The only one who will make you a SUCCESS is YOU!"

Tricks for learning to achieve success.

Vision - Structure – Determination

The Unseen Sight!

"Do you want what I have?" uttered David Blaine. "What "D" a carbonated water?" I sarcastically joked. David continued, "No I mean the success, the television shows, and the whole business. I know you do. I can see the drive in you.

No one gave me this. I had no one handing me my first television show. I had to make them believe in me. Scott... No one is going to believe in you but you. No one is going to make you a success but you. "

the ATTACK PLAN

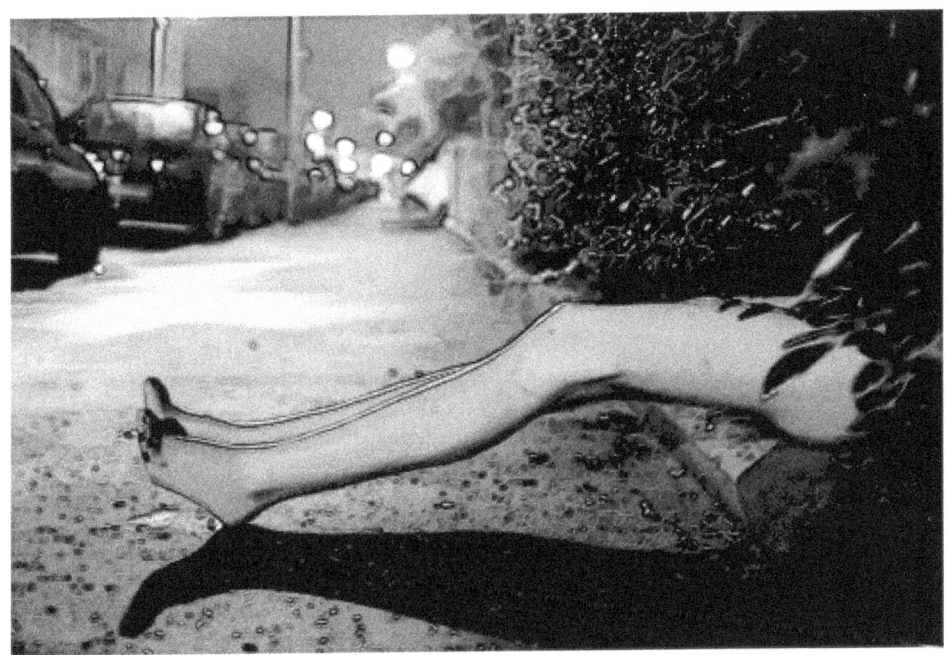

the **Effect:**

From General Ulysses S Grant to George Patton, the leaders and warriors who have succeeded in winning have always shared a secret knowledge. They knew that with intelligence, planning, and a plan of attack that they could regulate the resources under then and achieve greatness.

Many great warriors throughout history, never liked the advent of new "revolutionary" mechanized weapons. Sir Douglas Haig of World War 1, preferred his mounted cavalry troops to attack in multi pronged attacks. Haig also was known for attacking early which left his opponents, and often his own men, off guard.

What do these war generals and leading professionals like David Blaine, Bill Gates, and even Donald Trump know about business?

the **Secret:**

All good ideas start with a vision. Unfortunately most stop there too because of poor business strategy and vision.

Success and vision go hand in hand. Try structuring your project using a flow chart and a business plan. These should be structured to highlight all obstacles and hurdles you may encounter. Have a counter plan of attack for each of these.

Imagine your business plan to be a strategic attack plan. All good generals have a stratagem for winning a battle. Focus your plan on your weapons for success.

Allow this plan to drive you. Every day take another task and achieve it. This should be a basic rule to all business success. Everyday take one step closer to your goals. The following will set up some very important answers that will be needed for the rest of this book.

Questions to ask yourself about your business for your attack plan:

1. How is my good/service different from the others on the market?
2. Why should my clients buy from me?
3. Who are my potential clients?
4. Where do my customers reside. Where do they shop, live, work, and play?
5. What are the most effective forms of exposure for my good/service? What advertising would help my product to succeed?
6. Are there any legal issues I may face?
7. Do I need special licensing or other governmental sanctions?
8. Which of your business associates can you delegate tasks too?
9. Set goals for each part of your plan.
10. Always have an exit strategy. Never put all your eggs in one basket! Remember there will always be slow times. So have a safety net and plan accordingly.

The more structured you become the easier it will become to set and achieve your goal. The Iphone and other PDA like phones are a blessing for busy businessmen. Like many of you, my life happens at the speed of light or email anyways. Having my Iphone allows me to jot down ideas and notes as they come.

I consider my Iphone to be an extension of my business plan and often keep my plan on my phones notes section. Many of you may scoff at the $600 price tag of the Iphone, but it allows me to contact my clients immediately. I get traffic, weather, maps, custom directions, upload pictures to my website, update news for clients, sell tickets, and even respond to contracts immediately.

What tools do you have in your attack plan?

WHODOO VOODOO?

the **Effect:**

The witch doctor began mixing various herbs and oils inside of a mojo bag. He said this concoction would protect me and aid in my fighting of diabetes while also promoting prosperity. I was skeptical… But do you know it work…

That whole week I kept that mojo bag close, my blood sugars were in check, and it seemed like good fortune was abound. How does the casting of spells and the belief in prayer work?

the **Secret:**

I am sure many will argue with me about my beliefs on this one. I am not going to argue about whether religions are right or wrong, nor will I speculate which deity is the true one. Instead this is about the psychology and science behind spells and prayers.

Think about the basics of casting a spell or a prayer. What happens? There's usually some intricate ceremony that ends in some physical or mental token created to help aid in whatever goal you have.

When you begin a prayer or cast a spell, you have your goal in mind. This means you are after something. By bringing that goal to the mind in a physical manifestation as a prayer or a spell, you get your mind set into the frame to succeed. You are in essence reminding yourself to achieve that goal. A little nagging and stress in one's life is sometimes a good thing.

So am I saying to go out and join a new cult or become a new age Wiccan and begin hugging trees? Goodness no!

Instead, why not get a piece of business equipment that you need and that will keep your mind focused on your goal. Sometimes by spending money on a new piece of equipment it encourages us to recoup the losses and achieve your success related goals.

This new piece of equipment now serves the same job as my mojo bag did. It keeps you thinking of your goals and sets your mind in the right frame set to achieve them.

the **Words of Wisdom**

the **Effect:**

During the first World- War, there was a story of a messenger on the front lines. This man was to carry a message: "Send reinforcements, we're going to advance…" Sounds straight forward enough, however by the time it reached the general it became: "Send three or four pence we are going to dance…"

Any message you communicate can get distorted and confused. But what is a good communication and how do you use it effectively?

the **Secret:**

As leaders in a goal to success, we need to be aware of how we transmit messages. Miscommunication happens because we inform our teams rather then communicate ideas with them.

Communicating an idea is the exchange of an idea that has the same meaning to those involved. By simply assuming your ideas are understood, you can fail in business.

If I asked you what is time, you may have an answer, which is completely different, then those around you. Time can be linear or a more general period of existence. The definitions are numerous.

If you are speaking of a specific genre or terminology, which a person is not familiar with, the idea also has the potential for becoming lost to the receiver.

When transmitting a message try to get feedback to ensure that your message was transmitted properly.

Next time you type an email, take a step back and read it. Try to find the meaning that it will carry. See it from the outside it. Don't just assume it will be understood. In this modern age of technology, message boards and emails are the number one avenue to get your business in trouble.

A friend of mine always states: "Write your email. Read it. Rewrite it, and then throw it away and rewrite it once again…" The key to success is being able to transmit ones ideas well and if you are stumbling for the right words, your competition might just get the edge over you.

When you telephone someone, ensure that you have written out your ideas thoroughly and know how to transmit them well. For cold calling have every avenue of conflict already mapped out and have a rebuttal for each. Never make it seem like an assault either. Just become a wise man with a solution for their problem!

"The gut you won't want to lose..."

Intuition as a fact not psychic pseudo-science.

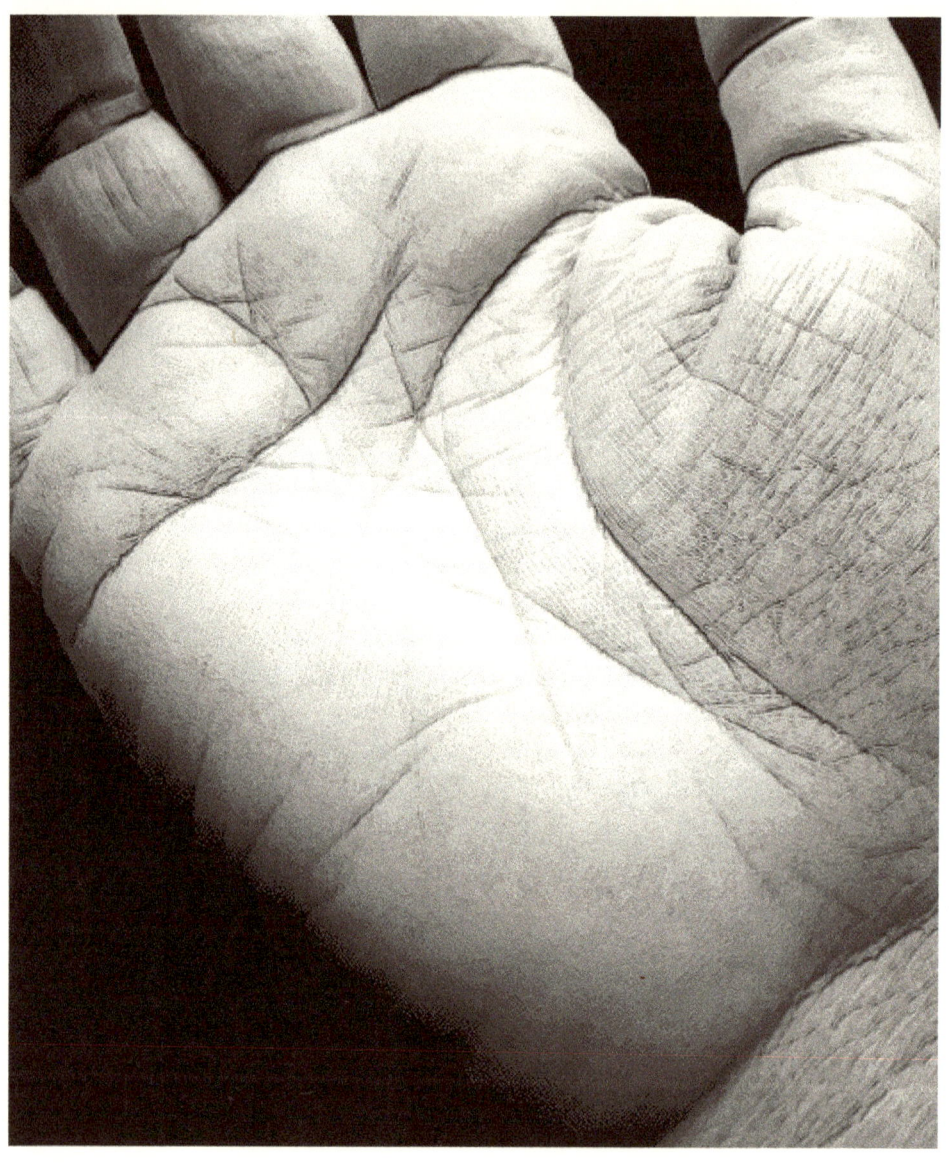

There exist moments in our life that we will never forget. The moment we saw our first love. The instant your child was born.

How about the moment when you heard a plane flew into the first World Trade Center tower? Where were you? How about when the second one was hit?

Do you remember the scene on television as the towers were hit? The smoke billowing from the open wound in the buildings. Remember the tragedy when both towers began to shake. Remember seeing the building explode, and fire rushing out, as they fell. Both of the towers falling down in unison mere seconds after the other.

How many of you actually remember seeing this? Well this is your intuition playing a trick on you. How? You were too focused on the details of the story.

The actual buildings never really cracked, nor did they fall in succession. They fell nearly 29 minutes apart. Nor, was there much of an explosion or fire as they came tumbling down. But, this didn't stop your mind from reading the details and focusing in on the details and crafting a false memory.

Lets try this again, with another example:

> *"You are driving a bus. The bus you're in leaves the bus station. At the first stop 8 people get on. 2 blocks later at the next stop 3 people get off 2 get on. At the next stop 2 people get off. Then the next stop 6 get on 1 gets off. At the next stop 4 more people get on. At the next stop 3 people get off."*

So how many stops were there? Better yet, who's driving the bus? Our senses act as a filter. Sometimes the important information we need is right there in our subconscious. This is intuition.

Elementary, my Dear Watson...

the **Effect:**

"It's elementary my Dear Watson." Those words were infamously tied to Sherlock Holmes. He always knew how a crime was committed. He could deduce who the criminal was. The time of death, as well as the instrument of death, was all a case of pure logic. To the untrained though, this seemed like real mind reading or intuition.

How can this be used in business?

the **Secret:**

The secret is to take in ALL the details from the world around you, and store it for later use. It's not magic that Sherlock Holmes and detectives can solve crimes. By gathering details from a scene, you can logically deduce the make up of that situation. Too often though, we do not even visualize the details from our everyday life.

Need an example?

"On your watch, are there numbers, Roman numerals, geographic shapes? At the 12 O'clock position, what's there? Your second hand, is it pointed?"

Only 60% of the people who will read this will know what indicators are on their watches, either numbers or numerals. Out of this only 40% will know what's in the 12 O'clock position.

Visualization exercise- Choose an object in the room around you, such as a pencil, book, etc. Hold it in your mind for a minute. Memorize all you can about it: What's it made from, where do the shadows fall, how does it feel in your hands, are there any words on it.

Now set the object aside and close your eyes. Recreate the object with all the detail you can in your mind. Take a pen and paper and begin jotting down all the details of that object. See just how many details you remembered, as well as how many you missed. In time your mind will begin doing this subconsciously, it just take active training.

Look up and make every day of your life a visual scene from a movie. Add as much detail to your memories as possible. Notice all the details about the room. Imagine your brain is a camera in your mind and take snap shots inside your mind of all the facts and details that make up that scene.

By training your mind, you open up your mind to collecting more facts and details for your intuition to process. In time you will notice more intuitive processing going on.

Stress, What is it Good for?

the **Effect:**

I worked 40-46 hours a week in college. On top of this exhausting workweek, I went to 2 colleges part time. You see, this was a cheaper way for an out of state resident to attend college full time. I had so many obligations such as rent and school tuition payments that I don't believe I ever slept. I passed school with a 3.2 GPA and barely ever went other then to turn in assignments and to take tests. I learned a secret that many have never known. Stress can be a powerful ally.

the **Secret:**

Stress and nervousness are in fact a form of intuition. Your body produces stress as a motivator to accomplish certain tasks. That's why you shouldn't consider it to be a negative.

Your body interprets all that subconscious information from the world around you and lets you know that you need to hype up the game and even sometimes to be careful. Stress and nervousness can be the most pure form of intuition and there's even more ways to turn it's effects into a more positive effort.

Make stress your friend! Your body has a natural fight or

flight reaction when in stressful situations. This produces many performance and energy enhancing chemicals, such as adrenaline, and that burst of energy will enhance your performance at the right moment. All great athletes and celebrities get nervous and stressed at times. Use stress wisely to push yourself a little bit harder at the moments when it counts most.

If the stress and nervousness gets too much, you can trick your body into relaxing by using heavy breathing. Breathe in slowly for a count of 6 then breathe out for a count of 10. This mild hyperventilating actually causes your body to become relaxed in moments of anxiety.

"Mind Reading"

Know your what your customers are thinking, and how to use this mind reading for corporate success and increased sales!

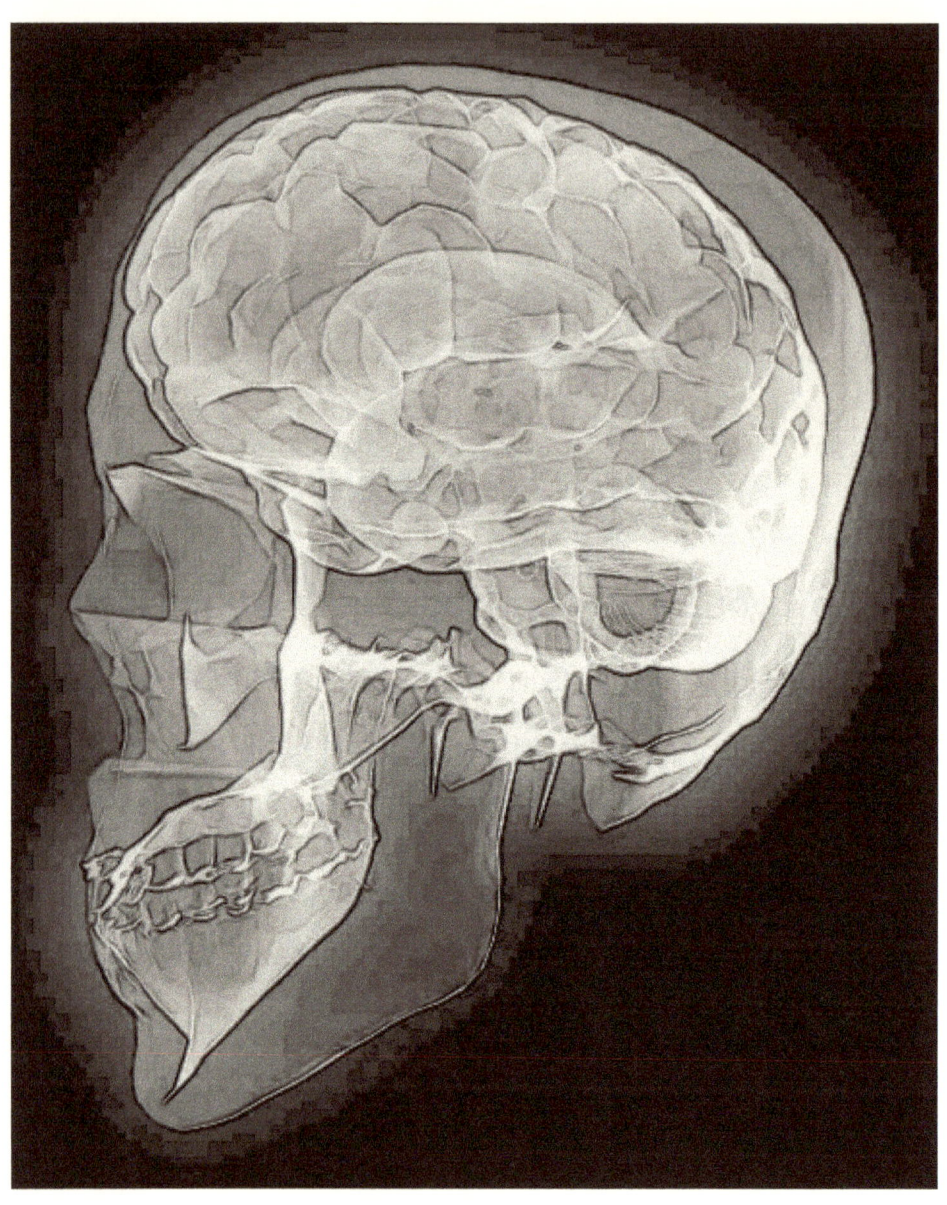

I looked at her and I could read her complete life. I told her about her father had left her, and now she feels resentment and even a little lost. I told her about her 2 loves in her life and how the one she truly loved had been more of a child then a willing adult in the relationship. She began to cry and admitted that I was touching things in her life that I shouldn't be.

Ever since that day, I have been giving intuitive readings and creeping everybody out, even myself. Is it really psychic to read minds? Not so much, instead it's more of a Sherlock Holmes process and being able to understand what people are saying, without them saying a single word.

Mind Reading

the **Effect:**

Imagine being able to look at your customers or even your friends and being able to know whether they are lying to you or not. Now imagine the potential of telling when someone is irritated, having a bad day, or even when they are excited about a deal. All this is a skill of a trained mind.

the **Secret:**

Body language is the unconscious mind causing involuntary reactions to happen within our bodies. These are called idiosyncratic reactions. When you know how and what to look for, the benefits especially in business, becomes obvious.

When an individual gets nervous, especially due to lying, the idiosyncratic reactions take over. When some one lies, their pulse rate becomes elevated, the rate at which they blink their eyes increases, nervous traits such as tapping of a foot or finger begin, body weight shifts, and when the liar invents a story the eyes will involuntarily look up and to the right. When you are asked to recall an event, a real memory that you have witnessed, your brain is programmed in such a way that you unconsciously tell your eyes to look up and to the left. While when you lie, or make up a story, the opposite reaction happens. When you lie, your eyes look up and to the right.

These techniques of lie detection have been employed by police officers and polygraph examiners for years. In fact the polygraph machine, or lie detector, uses your rate of breathing, pulse, and perspiration to tell when you are lying and telling the truth. Of course con men also know of these techniques and use various counter techniques to cause false positives and inconclusive findings in the polygraphs.

NLP Thought Detection

Expanding on the information above, Neuro-Linguistic Programming (NLP) can be used to detect basic thoughts. People use three major modes of thinking: visual, auditory and kinesthetic. Communicating in the mode of the other person can help you gain rapport and improve the exchange of information.

Using eye movements that are subconsciously created through the brains idiosyncratic techniques, you can easily detect what an individual is thinking of.

Visual mode
In the visual mode, the person thinks of a visual memory. By observing the person's eyes, sometimes that person will gaze upward to the left slightly. These eye movements are an indication

of thinking in a visual mode.

Auditory mode

In the auditory mode, the person thinks of the memory of hearing sounds. Such is the case when thinking of the memory of a favorite song. By observing the person's eyes, you will notice that they will often look sideways to the left and horizontal to the ground.

Kinesthetic mode

In the kinesthetic mode, the person thinks of a memory of emotion and feeling. By observing the person's eyes, you will notice that they will often look down and to the left.

Mental process

When you ask a person a question, he or she may answer by recalling some event or by logically determining or creating the answer. This creation of a memory will follow the same eye movements but rather the eyes will focus on the opposite direction to the right.

Lying with Their Eyes

When inventing a visual image, the eyes are drawn up and to the right. As with sounds horizontal and to the right will denote an invented sound or conversation. Emotions are down and to the right.

Additionally lies often follow uneasy body language and

nervous behavior. A twitching of the eyes will show a need to invent an image in the mind. Stuttering and hesitation in speech also show a nervous behavior, and should be taken as a sign of lying.

the **Psychic Detective**

the **Effect:**

Imagine the power of being a real psychic and know how much a customers business is truly worth, how much their home is worth, the name of their wife and kids, and even the birth date of his whole family. What an amazing marketing angle to "mind read" such personal details, and even have a birthday cake delivered on his wife's birthday. Who's going to get his business this year?

the **Secret:**

This is secret I use often when working with new clients. A simple website known as cisworldwide.com will allow you to run intricate background searches for a one time fee. The more complex a request you desire, the more chance you will need to up the search to a premium level which will cost a few dollars more.

The idea of being able to know the clients personal information can allow you to slide by some defense mechanisms that they may have in place. Imagine having a birthday pizza sent to your client's house on his son's birthday. This would be a memorable moment that would place your business in a favorable position. Also imagine being able to get detailed business earnings and property holdings for a clients business! Use this tool wisely and the gates to business success will be bountiful.

Never admit to how you are doing these tricks. Always just smile and let them know you are a man of mystery who has some tricks up his sleeves. This creates a persona of mystery, and courts your clients with an aura of excitement.

the Cold Read

Of course knowing when someone is lying helps, but there are other techniques that allow you to tell the thoughts of a person. Using techniques such as "Cold Reading", the technique of the psychic readers to read certain "tells" of an individual that reveal inner information about them without ever meeting them before, it becomes evident that our lives are open books to skilled readers.

Because of our status in life, and our careers, we develop various postures, swaggers, and reactions to scenarios. Depending on our age, readers can make educated guesses about events that are happening around us. Whether we are married, if we have children, if we are in school, or whether we have jobs are all key factors to finding out who we are to a "psychic reader."

Sometimes, as is the case with most gypsy readers, they do this unconsciously. This is what professionals call "shut eyed" readers, or professionals who do not realize that they are performing "cold readings" unconsciously. The other type of psychic is the most devious kind, "Open Eyed" reader. These men use the techniques of cold reading and psychology knowing exactly what they are doing. They often place the title "psychic" on what they are doing claiming that they are highly intuitive.

Some unscrupulous "psychics" use this gift to defraud other

naive individuals out of their money; such is the case with psychic surgeons in the Philippines.

As your first exercise I would like you to make a note of the body language of your friends and family's. For the next two or three days watch everything they do and how they do it. It might help to keep a spiral notebook of these actions. As you start developing a crib sheet of those around you, you realize that certain people act the same way. These people are usually in the same social class or career. Even those in your family may not have the same body language due to the language they learn from those around them at school or work.

Keep a note of their eye movements when they are asked a question. Learn the way they walk. Watch the way they learn. Watch them when they are happy, sad, content, and excited. Now try asking them to think of one real event in their life. Now have the individual tell you the one real event, but mix it some where between two other stories that are fictional. Try to decipher through their body language which of the two stories are fictitious.

By knowing the signs of body language especially when someone is lying, you can subtly tell what they're thinking. True this isn't the earth shattering secrets that some pseudo-psychics would have you believe, but this is as close to telepathy as I have seen. In fact the worlds best mind readers and psychics use this very technique.

"Ultra Memory"

Never forget a name, date, or fact ever again!

the Secret of Memory

the **Effect:**

The power of a trained memory is perhaps one of the most devastating powers anyone can have in their arsenal for business. You will be able to remember dozens of names not to mention countless business numbers and contacts.

So what is the most special word to an individual, their own name.

the **Secret:**

So what's the secret to an "Ultra Memory"? Well I hate to say it but its repetition. It also doesn't hurt to incorporate visualized imagery and mnemonics. Well let me break it down for you.

The mind of a usual individual is like an office with files thrown everywhere. In this chaos, how are you ever going to find anything? The first step is to turn each and every memory into a visual representation. That is any information you need to remember has to be made into an image.

Why you may ask? Our mind stores and recalls data in images. I know you hear a little self-dialog in your mind, that's normal. But, if I asked you to think of your couch you wouldn't think of the words red, black, stripes, about 3.50 feet tall, etc. You would recall the image of the couch and then the inner dialog would process the information for speech purposes.

Once you have the images visualized, we have to give that office some order, a mental bookcase of sorts. I will teach you a pegging system for order. A pegging system is a numbered list (a constant, unchanging) that will allow you to attach the needed memory and recall it at will. The first thing we will need to make is the rudimentary system. I will describe a simple body pegging system I created, while watching another mentalist's television special.

In this special, Mr. Derren Brown describes an imaginary office in his mind that he pegs information in for later memory demonstrations. I decided it would be easier to better organize it into a list that is easily accessibly visibly, namely the human body.

There are more complex lists and I would highly recommend learning one, but for space and copyright reasons, I have made a simple pegging system so you can remember a list of several items easily.

Memory List:
1. Toes
2. Feet
3. Ankle
4. Knees

5. Hip

6. Abdomen - Waist

7. Chest

8. Hands

9. Shoulders

10. Head

Notice how the body-pegging list corresponds to their respective position, as they would appear on the human body. Obviously you could continue making a more detailed list, but for a quick demonstration I have chosen to keep it brief. Now the key is to attach your list to the items you need to remember, and to do this with as much action as possible. The more action involved, the better the memory will stick. Since our brains are wired to think visually, this action becomes mental glue.

The more detail and story based action you give to your individual memories and the pegging visual, the easier it will be to recall the information later.

Example:

You have a list of 10 items to get from the grocery store. First item is grapes. An easy method for pegging this to our system would be to imagine an old Italian woman squishing grapes for win with her toes. So grapes would then be pegged to toes. Remember to add as much action as possible. Adding detail and texture in these mental visualizations can help! The second item on our list will be bandages. For this you might imagine a gapping wound on your foot (the second item of our pegging list) from walking too far. Thus by needing a bandage to cover it.

I didn't want this work to become a home memory course so I decided to keep it direct. The information above is more then enough to get you started to remembering almost anything. You may wish to make your own body list with more detail so that you can peg more information. What about names?

Memorizing Names:

The key to remembering names is to turn their names into images and peg them on the list. The name Chris I turn into a picture of a cross or Christ. The name Jennifer I might remember as a Gem. The possibilities are endless. I believe the only true work on memory you'll ever remember is your own. So I have given you the basic premise on the names and now I want you to make up your own visuals for names, thus by making it more personal and thus by making memory linkage easier.

Memorizing Numbers:

This technique works by building pictures in your mind, in which you represent numbers by things that rhyme with the number. Then once this is done, you link the numbers together to form a "visual" story in your mind. The visual aspect help "glue" it to your memory.

The more action you use the better your memory.

The usual rhyming scheme is:

1. Bun
2. Shoe
3. Tree
4. Boar
5. Hive
6. Bricks
7. Heaven
8. Gate
9. Mine (Land Mine)
10. Hen (Can also be used for zero)

If these images do not work in your mind, then change them for something that works. I am currently using a number word association that is not based on rhymes but rather on associations such as 5 and the words glove. The reason being a glove has 5 fingers. For the ease of memorizing, I will allow you to use the rhyme list and if you wish to create your own association list, then you can advance from there.

Remember the sillier the visual story image, the more effectively you will remember the number sequence.

For example, you could remember the number 7082688403 by imagining this story:

You see angels floating chatting in **heaven** as a cartoon **hen** slowly ascends. The golden **gates** of heaven open slowly as a blinding light shines in your eyes. The hens **shoe** falls off and lands just in front of the **bricks** of the **gates** of heaven. The **gates** then slam shut, as a pursuing **boar** tries chasing the **hen** up a **tree**.

Now imagine this story again and add details for all the objects within this story see the hens feathers and see all the details of the gate and the other key words. Once you have this story down, you will have remembered my phone number.

"Mind Control"

Create your own destiny, influence others,

& super charge your life.

What we perceive of the "world around us is done so through our five senses. We transform this data into electrical impulses that are interpreted in our brain. Reality is based in this very interpretation.

But, what of those chemicals, stimulants, and illnesses that alter those electrical impulses? Our universe and our very reality can change and be altered.

When you realize that drugs such as LSD can cause you to experience a garden of life in a simple shadow and that a dieing man can witness angels and demons, then you will realize that anything is possible in a reality that we ourselves create in our brain. The secret is taking control and shaping your existence.

In this book I show you how to create a new reality that will make you seem paranormal. You will learn to combat those annoying habits. You will be able to tell when those around you are lying. You will learn to influence people through positive actions that make you in control of every situation. You will become a master of the human mind!

The only one who can change your life and allow you to achieve your dreams is you. You will experience 75 summers and only you can create what capacity you will experience them in.

the **Mind Controller**

the **Effect:**

Paul was one of the most affluent and influential people to walk the Earth. He would walk into a room and light it up. Paul could get the phone number and better still, the attention, of any woman he met. He called upon his friends to help him with a task, and they all caved to his will. Paul has the ability to control minds.

the **Secret:**

The following are a list of everyday tactics to influence how people act. The minor details that follow can deeply impact your business.

Rule of Attraction:
As humans, we are attracted to pretty things. If you wish to control what people think, then you must attract their vanity. In business always look as good as the best customer you will encounter. You never want to scare them off by looking too rich and glamorous, the average client may worry about their pocket books.

Shoes are quite possibly the most over looked part of a wardrobe but convey the most. Men will often overlook their footwear, while women notice this detail. Always keep a clean and polished pair of shoes.

Accessories such as a fine watch, tie, and belt can make an average attire rise above the others. People are often attracted to shiny objects and do not even realize it. You are worth what your attire tells the client your worth. Remember that in evolution, the peacock with the biggest and brightest feathers always gets the mate.

Phone 101:
Contact is essential to all businesses. Always answer your business line. Voicemail sounds like a great idea but often clients will want their questions answered and in a timely manner. If you aren't doing this, the competition just might be. It might be effective to have a secretary or an answering service to take your calls and setting the customers minds at ease.

Remember to always be cordial on the phone and treat all your callers as guests. Be fair with what you require, but also ask for what you want from your clients. If you do not ask for something, you will never get it.

The number one secret you can use over the phone is to close every call with: "Hey thank you **STEVE** (or what ever their name is) for calling". This once again uses the memory technique of remembering the clients name, thus by showing importance of the name, and produces the number one sound ever client likes to hear, their own name. You also use an old adage that every conman understands; you make it seem as if they are helping you and as such bolster their ego's making them feel good. Give this closing technique a try and reap the rewards.

Time is a Precious Commodity:
Those objects which are often just outside our reach is the most sought after. Be sure to be seen and available, but don't be too much of a nuisance. No one ever likes the used car sales man as they're too over baring. Make your presence known but never seem too anxious and needy as these seem like acts of desperation.

Eye Contact & Personal Space:
Always make eye contact with your clients. This act conveys an alpha-male approach. This also breaks down the cold harsh first contact and opens up initial contact. Also a subtle touching of the arm of a client opens up the personal space and subconsciously all you to be a closer personal friend.

Be Where the Clients Are:
Be where your clients are. By being in the same circles, you become their friend. Friends like to buy from friends. The more you are seen, the more you are a part of the circles and the easier it is to purchase you commodity.

Win ANY Argument:

Sometimes everybody will come into a confrontational person who will just want to argue. How can you win any argument? Simply ask the aggressor/opponent, what they want from you. What do they expect from you? Can you give this to them? And if not, express why you cannot and come to a better expectation, which is a better solution for the both of you. Often what the aggressor wants is less then what you are willing to give. Never give more then you have to...

Suggestion and Persuasive Language

the **Effect:**

It has been said that some world leaders such as Hitler have possessed the ability to hypnotize their audiences using their words. Normal rational people are thrust to follow celebrities and politicians due to an unseen force.

the **Secret:**

The old adage goes: *"Its not what you say its how you say it."* There exists a subtlety that many overlook, suggestion. Too often people talk at you rather then influencing you with words.

Inflection, or verbal force and excited tonnage, is a very powerful tool. Due to evolutionary processes, the control and range of our voice often causes emotions and even control in audiences.

I would like you to listen to those friends and co-workers around you. Listen to how they emphasize certain words, especially when they need (I know it's sometimes a subjective term) something from you.

As humans we have been bread to act to stimuli a certain way. By adding inflection to important words, you help deliver your point across quicker and harder. Next time you have something important to say write it down first and find the action words to emphasize. Remember to never stall or stutter as our audiences look upon those two actions negatively.

Exercise Time:

In the following sentence notice the words that are bold. Say the sentence normally, and then try saying it a different way by adding excitement and bolder strength to the words that are in bold text.

"I would like to **speak** with you about the **new** budget." Or "I would **like** to speak with you about the **new** budget."

Try them both. There's no right or wrong answer. The goal is to carry your goal across quicker and harder hitting. See what you can come up with. After you have tried all combinations of inflection, try them for a trusted friend. See if they can help you learn a cleaner and more effective way to carry across your message!

Performing for audiences is covered with nuances of speaking such as the example above. An important part of what you say is the words that you are speaking. I want you to imagine the word odor. What visual came to mind? If you are like most humans the idea of garbage or some particular bad smell comes to mind. Now think of an aroma. What comes to mind? You'll probably think of sweet perfume or other delectable fragrance. I am a firm believer in that one word can influence a whole conversation.

In business keywords should be found that carry across your point.

Could you imagine speaking about the odor of a new clients cookie? The looks of disgust on your audience, especially if the cookie manufacturer is present, would quickly become apparent. A good idea is to always write down every important point you need to convey before you need to convey it. Find action-grabbing keywords that will better help describe your subject. If I would have known this back in high school, the power of vocabulary, I could only imagine the powerful essays and book reports I could have written!

Hypnosis History:

"How to use your mind to change your existence."

All hypnosis is a form of self-induced hypnosis. This is why self-hypnosis to change you behavior or habits will not work unless you truly want top change. By reading this book you are showing initiative to change, and that is a positive first step. If you are being forced to read this, I give you permission to stop reading. You will never gain anything from this book if you are forced to read it.

There is no mystic force or power behind hypnosis. The evil Svengali figure that we have preconceived in our minds simply does not exist. Everything that I have learned from the numerous courses I have attended, the many friends (I despise the word clients especially in such a symbiotic relationship as hypnotist and client) I have helped, and the hundreds of books I have read suggests that hypnosis cannot force you to do something you are not morally or ethically inclined to do normally. I do not know what evil chemicals the government top mind scientists are cooking up, but as for the hypnosis used in clinics and stage hypnotists their power lies in YOUR mind and its desires to change states.

This is why a desire and interest to change is essential for self-hypnosis to work. You desire to be a better you, a superhero of sorts. Not all superheroes have great powers. Most only have one special something that sets them apart. You see or soon will see an avenue of your life that is lacking, and soon you will compensate for this personality trait and turn into a better **SUPER YOU**.

If you are ready to change into a better **NEW** you, lets begin.

Hypnosis Overview:

As all complete books of any subject should, I will delve into the history of the subject material (hypnosis).

- You will meet the men who shaped hypnosis into its modern state.
- The exploration of the trance and the myths surrounding it.
- Self evaluation of yourself and inner perceptions of what you desire to change and detecting that which triggers the undesirable trait.
- Changing and stopping triggers from happening and changing outer perceptions.
- Visualization.
- The secret to hypnosis & inducing a trance.
- Practical evaluations and procedures of self-hypnotic techniques.
- Communicating and seduction tips
- Claustrophobia
- Lose weight

Overview of the Xavier hypnotic method:

In the Beginning-

The idea of hypnosis and its use as a positive development change in an individual's life has been around since the dawn of time. The first record of hypnosis is found in the bible, the book of Genesis 221-22 (ASV) states, "So the Lord caused a deep sleep to fall upon man, and while he slept took one of his ribs and closed up its place with flesh; and the rib which God took from the man, he made into woman and brought her to the man." Hypnotists have shown that this passage is a form of the modern use of using hypnosis as an anesthesia.

Other ancient sources of hypnotic references are those found in Ebers Papyrus, a more then three thousand year old Egyptian scroll. This ancient Manuscript describes a unique place of healing called Egyptian "Sleep Temples."

These temples housed Egyptian priests who would use a hypnotic-like procedure to implant suggestions for healing and health. The temple became so popular that they eventually spread to ancient Greece and Asia Minor!

Having its basis in the bible and sleep temples, it isn't so hard to believe that one of the earliest pioneers in hypnosis was not a physician but rather a clergyman. Father Gassner, a catholic priest who lived at Klosters, hypothesized that patients who were ill were possessed by the devil and demons. And only once these demons were cast out could the subject attain a state of good health.

Having gained church approval by claiming that God was working through him, Gassner allowed physicians of the time to witness his experiments. Rather then being a modern procedure. Timing his entrance to make the most of the spectacle, finding the physicians seated around a stage in which the patient was on "display". Father Gassner was quite the showman. In a theatrical flowing black robe, Gassner strolled onto the stage with a golden crucifix in hand.

The patient had been implanted with a suggestion. The suggestion was that when Father Gassner touched him with the crucifix, he would promptly fall to the floor and wait for further instructions. Gassner's patients were then told to alter their minds into believing that they would "die." In this state of altered reality, Gassner would cast out the demon, and then from this point on they would be cured. Doesn't this seem like a little mind over matter?

The physicians were invited to examine the patient and felt no pulse, heard no heart, and believed the patient to be dead, and then Gassner would demand that the demon depart, and shortly thereafter the patient would spring back to life cured. The subtlety of hypnotic suggestions and strong under tones of religious conviction were surely behind these miraculous feats.

Franz Anton Mesmer was an Austrian physician, who witnessed Gassner's unique demonstrations. Scientifically speaking, Mesmer is credited with the discovery of modern hypnosis, and is widely acknowledged as the 'Father of Hypnosis'. He believed that there was a magnetic fluid in the very air we breathe and that the body somehow absorbed this fluid. Mesmer considered disease to be caused via a blockage of the circulation of this magnetic fluid in the blood. Mesmer went on to hypothesize that to cure a patient; you must cure the blockage of these magnetic fluids.

Treatments initially used a magnet, and later his hand, which was passed over the diseased body in an attempt to unblock the magnetic flow. The hand and the eyes were believed to unblock the fluid and increase the magnetic flow over the blocked areas. This belief in a magnetic flow was the origin of the term "animal magnetism" as well as the procedure "Mesmerism".

The Marquis de Puysegur was a pupil of Mesmer's. Puysegur utilized Mesmer's techniques of "animal magnetism" on a young peasant who entered into a state of trance like sleep, yet the peasant was still able to communicate with Puysegur and respond to his commands or suggestions. Once the peasant was awake, he remembered nothing of the session. Puysegur thought that psychological influences, especially in the hypnotist's actions, were extremely important in the whole process.

Time has not always looked positively at the practice of hypnosis or mesmerism. At the University College of London John Elliotson (1791-1868), an English physician who held a chair at the University was disbarred from the medical profession as a direct result of his demonstrations of animal magnetism.

Still the medical community was divided as to the usefulness of mesmerism around the period of the late 1840's. James Esdaile, a surgeon was operating on his patients using mesmerism as his sole anesthetic.

James Braid (1795-1860), a noted Scottish surgeon working in Manchester, was the first to coin the phrase "Hypnosis". Braid found that subjects could easily enter a trance like state simply by staring at a shiny object such as a pocket watch.

Braid also believed that some sort of neuro-physiological process was involved with hypnosis. Braid found hypnosis very useful in disorders where no organic origin to the problem could be identified such as migraines and headaches. He found that a post-hypnotic suggestion or rather a single word was enough to re-hypnotize a subject. Physicians such as Braid and his colleagues were at a loss as to how hypnosis actually worked, although many had some theories.

Jean-Martin Charcot (1825-1893), was a leading neurologist

and head of the neurological clinic at Saltpetiere in Paris, who used hypnosis to treat hysterics who we're found to be prone to fits and seizures.

Hippolyte Bernheim (1837-1919), a professor of medicine at the University of Nancy concluded that hypnosis was a special form of sleeping where the subject's attention is fixated upon suggestions made by the hypnotist. Bernhein reemphasized the neuro-physiological connection to hypnosis that Braid made.

In the mid - 1920s, hypnosis became the focus of strenuous experimental investigation. Clark L. Hull a leading psychologist demystified hypnosis saying that it was essentially a part of normal human nature. Hull also found that certain subjects were more suggestible and hypnotizable then others. The major factor was their imaginations.

In 1955 the British Medical Association set forth the standards of medical and therapeutic teaching of hypnosis. In 1958 the American Medical Association soon followed their British counter parts.

Recently, Milton H. Erickson, M.D. (1901-1980) has been credit with being the leading authority on clinical hypnosis. Erickson was a highly effective psychotherapist, devised countless innovative and creative ways to treat his patients using the basis of hypnosis. Erickson was a master of indirect hypnosis, and often used metaphor, surprise, confusion and humor to entrance his patients.

The Xavier Self Hypnosis Method:

The Trance:

The basis of all hypnosis is the trance. What is a trance? The trance is an altered state of consciousness. What does that mean? Think of the state you are in now. When that state changes it is altered. So any state that has changed from the moment before it, is an altered state. Our goal is to find a way to make this "altered state1' a positive one and control what it will influence.

When you learn the basics of hypnosis you will learn that it is quite easy to enter a trance and to use these trances for positive development for your beneficial growth as a being, basically to help achieve you goal of being that idealistic Super You. The benefits of such a trance are endless. Most notably learning and perception are heightened inside of the hypnotic trance state. The benefits to a student or even to an individual trying to lose weight soon become apparent.

Inner Evaluation:

As humans, it is evident that we all have flaws. Many of which are psychological in nature, while others are physiological. With the Xavier method of self-hypnosis we will concentrate on trying to help alleviate the inner demons of the self-perceived psychological flaws.

Obviously if you are reading this, you have some flaw you are in need of change. Whether it is losing weight, stop smoking, or just being more affluent in a social scene you will have to have a goal in mind.

Try and take a step out side of your life. Find a role model. Is there someone you wish to be more like? Is there a personal hero of yours? This individual will possess the characteristics (or super powers as in our earlier example) you wish to have in order to be the new Super You. This trait can be anything from not smoking to being a ladies man; the decision as to what to change is a private one you must find.

Once you have your super-goal in mind. You must evaluate your personal flaw that you desire to change. The first question involved in the evaluation process is what causes this undesirable trait? Bring into your consciousness that which is normally seen as unconscious.

If your undesirable trait is claustrophobia, you must find the triggers, which trigger the feelings of anxiety. Do the walls appear to close in on you? Are there any visual markers that cause you to get claustrophobic? Is your personal space feeling as if it's being invaded? How far away is it when this fear happens? Which spaces cause you to feel this anxiety? Are there any close spaces that do not bother you and why?

I will use another example of over eating. What are the triggers for over eating? Do you feel as if you're hungry? Does boredom set in? Is eating a crutch for you? Does eating fill time in your life? Is food the answer to social problems? Does food make you feel better? These are your triggers, the traits that trigger the desire to do the undesirable.

See the proceeding sections for specific triggers on the following: Stop Eating, Lose Weight, Be a Better Communicator & Learn to Seduce, and a general method of motivating positive developments. .

Self Evaluation:
Once you have found the source of your undesirable activity. You must find a way to attack, that which causes the undesirable reactions. We will view this as the Kryptonite for your undesirable trait.

Perhaps the easiest way to understand would be to use the example of over eating. As many Americans are realizing, over eating is a serious problem. The triggers we over viewed above are our villains to overcome.

Many of my friends who I have hypnotized have stated a

strong urge to eat due to a feeling of boredom. So what's the Kryptonite for this villain of boredom? There are several.

The first step is to become aware every time this trigger happens. The awareness process may first seem hard to get the hang of, but if you are truly wanting of change and willing to change then it you will work at this goal.

Eventually it will become a second nature habit to notice and detect the triggers. When you notice a trigger, pause for a moment. Take the extra second of time to ask yourself how to avoid the trigger. Develop a method to interrupt this scenario. This known as a pattern interrupt in hypnosis, and by distancing yourself for the trigger, you are in essence altering your state of consciousness. Thus by starting the trance process. Is there an activity you can be doing rather than eating?

Visualization:
The key to practical working hypnosis is visualization. Visualization is the way the mind works. If I said the word DOG to you, you would think of a visual representation (picture) of a DOG. You would not think in letter the word, DOG. This is why it is so important to use "visualization" for you to change.

Most people visualize so well that they are not aware that they are doing it. In fact the reason we believe we think in words is because the flashes of imagery are gone almost instantaneously and converted to cognitive words. We train our minds to think in a logical manner i.e. words. How would a deaf person who had never been exposed to images think, in pictures? In fact the blind individuals of the world are said to visualize that which they touch mentally, thus creating a 3-D representation in their minds.

An important thing that you first realize about visualization is that it is not limited to mere images and pictures. It encompasses many other senses. Visualization may contain the voice of your significant other. The smell of your mothers meat loaf cooking is also visual. The texture and feel of sand paper is yet another example of visualizing. All the tastes you've experienced.

Visualization is the whole experience of sights, sounds, smells, tastes and touches. The key to making hypnosis work is strong visualization.

Since learning to visualize is such a large part of hypnotic success, it is essential to learn new methods to better visualize. Take a look at your wristwatch; if you do not wear a wristwatch make it a wall clock. Now close your eyes and try to see the watch in your mind. How clear of a picture did you create? Now open your eyes and really observe you watch.

Notice all the details about the wristwatch. View the minute and hour markers. The hands of the watch. The stem, does it pull out or unscrew? Are there any scratches on the watch? Notice where the watch is in space. Notice where it isn't. Visualize the dimensions of the watch.

Notice how much easier it is to keep the watch's image in mind when you visualize the detail.

Now let's try creating a new visualization. Let's try to visualize a ball. Let's Visualize/imagine a white ball on a black background. Now invert the image and make it a black ball on a white surface. Does it cast a shadow? Is the background a room? Is the room detailed at all? What's the ball made of? Make it a super ball which bounces all cross the room. Add details of the course it takes. Does it have a trail as it bounces? Does it make a sound as it bounces? Now change the ball to a steel ball. Now bounce the ball. Did it make a visual transition to the steel ball, and if so what did the transference look like? Does the bouncing of the steel ball leave damage to the background? What sound does it make now. Are there any smells?

The Induction:
The induction is the method of being put under hypnosis or in our case self-hypnosis. Creative visualization is our method and basis of induction. We are going to try distancing our selves from the earlier stated triggers through implanting suggestions and the use of the visualization induction. Simply follow the script below and visualize in depth and detail every action. Believe what you are reading is really what you are experiencing. Please read this book

thoroughly before attempting the induction script.

The Script-

Aside:
You should be seated or laying a comfortable position. You should be wearing comfortable loose fitting clothing as well.

Take a deep breathe through your nose and hold it in for 6 seconds. Now, through your mouth, exhale completely and slowly. Continue breathing long deep breaths through your nose and exhaling through your mouth. Focus on your breathing. Become aware of it. Visualize each breath. Tense up all your muscles. On the count of ten to one, release them slowly, you will find them very relaxed.

Now close your eyes. Continue feeling and visualizing each breath. The depth and length of each breath is becoming constant and regular. As you lie there with your eyes comfortably closed you find yourself relaxing more and more with each moment and breath. The relaxation feels deep and tingly. You happily give way to these wonderful feelings. Imagine a blanket caressing your body. The blanket and the tingling sensation begin to work its way within and without your toes.

The blanket continues moving; it slowly moves up your feet, making them warm, heavy, and relaxed. The blanket is soft and supports your body with its soft texture, the gentle engulfing of the blanket is relaxing, and the peacefulness absorbs you completely. The tingling gentleness and warmth of the blanket moves up your leg, relaxing them. Making them warm and heavy. The relaxation feels very exquisite. You feel so good and pleasant at rest. Just relax and let go.

As the tingling continues its journey up into your body you feel your stomach muscles become very relaxed. Now, it moves slowly into your chest. On the count of 4 you will awaken again, stronger and energized. 4 you are feeling inner strength. Take a deep breath and exhale. 3 you are relaxed and at peace. Take another breath and release. 2 you are awakening and your feeling energized. 1 you are awake, wide-awake and feeling great!

This is your Zen place. Nothing bothers you hear. When you are in need of It, simply think "Zen Place" and see yourself distancing from the triggers and problems of the undesirable trait. Simply reaffirm the changes you need and have previously explored under the prior section of self-evaluation. You will feel the inner confidence grow and the "Zen Place" will no longer be needed.

Once you have mastered the concepts and have memorized the basic script. It will be necessary to confront that which is causing the anxiety or undesirable trait.

Begin the basic induction script and attain a strong and deep trance state. Once here, your goal will be not to distance yourself but rather to intercept the undesirable trait. You will in essence send yourself into a position in which you will experience that undesirable trait.

When you've mastered the basic script and "Zen Place" visualizations, it should be obvious on how to construct more scenarios. Once you are in one of these scenario's that places you in the undesirable position, I want you to Continue Script-

You are at peace, totally relaxed, and feeling more at peace then you ever have before. The warmth engulfs you. As this warmth engulfs you the image begins to dissolve into your "Zen Place." You are at the beach (Or where ever your Zen Place may be this is merely an example) and you lay comfortably on a folding beach chair. You feel the warmth of the sun beating down upon you. You hear the seagulls as they fly near by. You notice the sand under you. You see the texture, the color, and the shapes that it makes.

There's a hill behind you. You cannot see over the hill. But you can see the detail of the hill. You can see the grass that makes it up. You feel a cool breeze consume you, and it feels good. The warmth of the sun once again consumes you. Two crabs scurry across the beach and you can hear the noises they make as they scamper by.

From now on, whenever you think to yourself "Zen Place" and imagine yourself distancing from scenario, you will visualize and be in this exact place, consumed by peace and relaxation. All anxiety slips away. There is no fear and anxiety in the "Zen Place."

When you feel comfortable and confident again, you will feel you're self-becoming strong. You are not anxious. You are confident. You are the opposite of your triggered undesirable trait. See yourself glowing with energy and power. Experience yourself getting stronger and consumed with energy. You will be prepared to distance yourself if needed from the said triggers, they no longer effect you.

Your breathing relaxed as well. The blanket and relaxation moves up your arms to your shoulders, your arms are heavy and relaxed. You are visualizing the complete relaxation you are feeling. You are pleasantly engulfed with relaxation and warmth. Now you can feel the warmth and engulfing of the blanket move into you face and head, relaxing your jaws, neck, and facial muscles. You have no worries or cares. You are completely relaxed and feeling warm and engulfed by this blanket of peace. You are completely at rest. Visualize your whole body the depth and dimension as the blanket is around you making you feel at rest, relaxed, pleasant, and warm.

Aside:

At this point you will be in an altered state from earlier, a state of heightened relaxation and visualization. This state is essentially hypnosis. Your mind has now been conditioned into a state of suggestibility. You have suggested that you are in a completely relaxed state. If you are feeling and visualizing this state, you are hypnotized. You may repeat this exercise to heighten the trance state, but it should not be necessary.

Now from the peace of the blanket I want you to create a Zen place. It is a place where you feel completely relaxed and at peace with yourself. This place is the farthest from your triggers and undesirable trait.

When you enter this Zen place the world cannot harm you. The traits do not exist here. You will visualize every aspect of this place that is far from your traits and problems. You feel at peace and relaxed. I will use a beach as a sample example for the Zen place for the continuation of the script.

Experience the triggers. But rather then giving in to them, distance your self from them. Make the traits powerless. It is your mind and you will control every aspect of this intercept reality. The visualizations become so strong, that they actually seem like reality to a degree. Begin to see and experience all the triggers on your list, and start to solve them one by one. The triggers no longer will matter to you. If the triggers end up growing stronger, distance yourself by concentrating on your breathing, relaxing, feel the warmth of the blanket over taking you, the triggers no longer exist, and go to your "Zen Place." Once in the "Zen Place", of course visualize everything in detail and reinforce the peace and relaxation feelings.

This Intercept Visualization scenario should be practiced as many times as it takes until you believe that you no longer fear or experience the anxiety of the triggers. When experiencing the scenarios for real try to become more aware of your inner strengths and opposites of the anxieties that you feel. When necessary go to the "Zen Place" and reaffirm your inner strengths.

This strengthening of your inner strengths and the external evaluations you previously explored will help you to condition your mind to accomplish your goals and turn you into that Super You that you desire to become! This is why a true desire to change is essential for hypnosis of any sort to work. The power is inside you.

Your problems, issues, undesirable traits are psychological. You are strong and can strengthen the positive, and distance and eventually remove the negative!

Communication & Seduction:

The power to communicate is the key to winning friends and is an influence in business as well as a key to everything we do. A master communicator influences others and develops relationships with them. Seduction is the subtleties we use as humans to influence others to communicate and develop a relationship with us, whether it is personal or business.

Inner Evaluation:

The triggers that cause an individual to be a bad communicator are numerous. Here are a few that can help bring those subconscious triggers into you consciousness so you can find their Kryptonite. You are a poor listener - Poor story teller - you lack interest - you mind wonders while being talked to - you are unapproachable - you are too nervous - you have a lack of confidence - you have poor hygiene.

Self Evaluation:

How can you be a better communicator? Visualize yourself doing some of the following. Show interest in subject material being discussed. Show your humanity; show your vulnerability to a point. Remember to be confident, you are important and will be listened to. Make eye contact. Nod at the "END" of every point. Match the conversation subject- Pace your voice to match theirs. Match your breathing to their breathing. Posture is an important part of making someone feel comfortable, by matching their vary posture they will feel more at ease with you.

Follow these examples and you will surely be a better conversationalist. These above methods are the very basis for seducing friends and business clients.

Visualizations:

Imagine you on a stage having a debate. Visualize all the mannerisms and traits your fellow debater possesses and match them. Come up with stories you can share about your life. Find interesting things in your life that you can share in case the subject matter ever dwindles.

Claustrophobia:
The feeling of claustrophobia is a very personal experience. The roots of such a psychosis can have real groundings in prior experiences that are extremely difficult to remove. When you realize this, you will be a lot closer to being able to find a way to combat it.

Inner Evaluation:
Only you know the true reason for you fears and what trigger them. Was there a particular experience that caused you to dislike enclosed spaces? Is it the distance of objects around you? Do the walls close in on you? Imaginary space seems to close in upon you?

Self Evaluation:
Find a way of searching inwards and distancing yourself from the enclosure. The walls no longer trap you. You are strong and can overcome these fears. Step back. You can visualize more room. The space isn't as small as it was before. There's nothing that can harm you about an enclosed space. It is a silly fear!

Visualization:

This is a perfect scenario to experience an imaginary journey on a cramped train or airplane ride. Experience all the triggers that trigger your anxiety. The closeness to the seat in front of you. The person next to you. The bad breath. Now distance yourself. The room around you is getting larger. It doesn't bother you. You are strong. Realize and believe that there is nothing in that room that can harm you.

Lose Weight:

Living in a society, which tells us that we must look like the models in magazines and on television, it's no wonder that millions of dollars a year are spent on losing weight.

Inner Evaluation:

What causes your desire to eat? Are there hunger pangs? Are you in cycle of eating? Do you lack energy to exercise? Are you eating just to fill time due to boredom?

Self Evaluation:

Visualize yourself not feeling those hunger pangs. Break and change any cycles, which cause undesirable eating. Even the slightest amount of activity to exercise is infinitely better then a whole world of non-exercise. Increase your activities and interaction with the world. Have a positive outlook on life. Distance yourself from the trigger of boredom eating. Also fill your time with more activities.

Visualization:

Experience the times in which you feel the desire to eat. Imagine the cravings or boredom triggers, and believe that they are diminishing they are becoming less and less because you are in charge of your mind and you body. Distance yourself from the triggers and visualize activities you could do to get more exercise. Walking the dog could be a form of simple exercise.

The Overview of the Xavier Induction of Positive Growth

You are a powerful being filled with the capacity for positive growth and change. Self-hypnosis is simply a tool to condition your mind into changing. Inner evaluation of your self is the first step to finding the answers. What triggers the undesirable trait, and finding that said trait, is your first and hardest step. Self- evaluation of the undesirable trait and steps to conquer it is the next hurtle you will have to overcome. By using the visualization tricks described you will be able to distance and eliminate the anxiety of the undesirable trait and thus by winning back your health and peace of mind. Find your "Zen Place" and use it as often as you need it, and whenever you find a minor flaw that needs improvement.

Advanced Thought Influence Concepts:

In the world, there are many ways to gain success. Below is a list of general theories that one should follow to become more powerful in a business sense. Manipulating a person's actions through your own influence allows you to be able to control any situation.

Manipulate those around you. Never put too much trust in friends, learn how to use your enemies:
Friends often feel lax in their position of being your friend. This is why you do not mix business with pleasure. Even the most trustworthy and hard working friend will become lax and laid back due to the fact that friendship is a buffer for their negative behavior. Friends may even betray you, for they are easily aroused to envy. They also become spoiled and tyrannical. Hiring a former enemy and he will be more loyal than a friend, because he has more to prove.

Better to keep your mouth closed and let people think you are an idiot, rather than opening your mouth and remove all doubt:
When you keep your plans to yourself, it creates an aura of mystery and power. It also makes it difficult for enemies to sabotage your plans. Keep people guessing and you will court their mysterious personality. Also by speaking less you create an air that you know more than you actually do.

Bait your enemies:
When you force the other person to act, you are the one in

control. It is always better to make your opponent come to you. Get them to strike first. When people react out of emotion, they leave all their carefully guarded walls behind. Entice your enemies and bait them with personal jabs. Know your enemy and get within their minds.

Actions speak louder:
You will always be remembered for your actions rather than winning an argument. Make others fear and respect you by making your actions speak for your personal moxie.

WAR what is it good for:
Personalities are infectious. If you are surrounded by negative personalities, then that is what you will become. Court those with whom are successful and you yourself will benefit.

Keep them hooked:
To maintain your independence you must always be needed and wanted. The more people need you, the more power you will possess.

Become their friends:
Throw off your enemies by becoming their friends. By showing positive actions to your enemies, you disarm them. This gives you the upper hand. This will also give you the ability to work

as a spy and gain subterfuge.

Complete destruction:
NEVER allow the enemy to come back and attack you. After your initial strike, make sure there is no room for them to strike back. Squash them completely!

Calculated insanity:
Court people's interests. By becoming unpredictable you court your fans fancy. While unpredictable, actions keep your enemies on guard, and keep them uneasy. This will ensure that they eventually snap and make a mistake.

King Kong ain't got nothing:
There are many different kinds of people in the world, and you can never assume that everyone will react to your strategies in the same way. Make sure you do not anger the wrong person. You do not need to start another battle.

Concentrate your forces:
Conserve your forces and energies for times of your choosing. Plan out your strategies and execute them at a time of your choosing. Make your efforts the ones that succeed, never fight on another's terms.

Re-create yourself:
Always recreate yourself. Keep people interested by reinventing yourself and your business.

Cleanliness is next to:
Get others to fight your battles. Make your friends and enemies battle for you. Never get your hands dirty as it muddies your reputation!

Best laid plans:
The ending is everything. Plan for all possible victories and defeat.

Oddball:
People believe in some strange things. Court their fancies and needs to believe in the obscene, and you will gain in the end.

Become royalty:
If you wish to have power, act like you have it. Make sure that you carry yourself and your plans with royal aspirations!

Focus, never get lost:
Be sure to have a goal in mind. Do not over burden yourself with too much. By adding trivial wants and aspirations to your life, you lessen what is really important.

Work on their hearts:
>Exploit peoples need to feel and care. Expose and utilize any weakness to make it a positive attribute.

Reflections:
>Show your enemies their own flaws. Exploit their weaknesses and prey upon them. Making an enemy look weak makes you look more desirable. But never do this on your own. Make their exploited weaknesses a product of their own actions and not your doing.

If you have read this book fully, you will now have the knowledge to achieve your goals in business. In my particular business of performing as a mind reader, the hardest thing I have to remember is that the hardest part of show business is the business. Never give up! Keep reaching for your dreams.

Remember:
>The only one who will make you a success is you...

Scott Xavier

www.ScottXavier.com

drzodiac@gmail.com

Scott Xavier *at a Glance...*

Some magicians pull rabbits out of hats.

Others, Mentalists, excel beyond the traditional sleight of hand and elevate into a category of entertainment that challenges the boundaries of reality... Scott Xavier - is one of the latter.

"I always hated the balloon clown magicians growing up," says Scott Xavier, "I like the unusual stuff that you hear about on television. The stuff that makes you uneasy and on edge. The stuff that just works even though no one knows whether it is real or not."

Scott Xavier of Plainfield, Illinois has showcased his stunts to corporate audiences all across the world. A self-described "mentalist," Scott Xavier combines elements of psychology, illusion, and theater to create a spectacle in which the audience is his chief canvas!

"I like creating an interactive environment where the freaky and strange demonstrations are happening in the audience and not to me, says Scott, who has been performing in nightclubs, colleges, and corporate events - he is also the mind reader for Kellogg's and Jamba Juice.

His techniques range from mental guessing games and

hypnosis to crowd-pleasing stunts, such as psychokinetic spoon bending and mind reading.

"There's a lot of twists and curves that are for everyone when I perform," he says.

Scott Xavier's show leaves traditional magic tricks behind and focuses on more elaborate schemes of popular psychology, verbal & non-verbal communication, intuition, & the paranormal.

"It's real mind reading! I can tell by the way someone's eyes wobble or by the direction their eyes are looking whether they are lying or not," he says. "By using clues such as this - and being observant - I can create some unique psychological demonstrations of mind reading and thought transference."

He says he has spent countless hours studying psychological techniques that allow him to guide people's thoughts and be attuned to subliminal clues that might reveal what they're thinking.

"We are all 98% alike, so when we're pressed to perform under pressure, we take the same preprogrammed actions," Scott states.

For Scott Xavier, the intersection from magic and the mind has been a lifelong pursuit. He earned a degree in Criminal justice and worked for a time in the Illinois State Police crime lab. But health problems - he is a diabetic - prompted him to chase his dream of becoming a professional "mentalist".

Growing up in Chicago's south side, Scott has been attracted to magic since the day he picked up his first magic trick at age 7 in a New Orleans magic shop. But when he was a teenager, Scott says, his relationship with occult changed.

At this point, he says, his uncanny ability to read people - he calls it the "Sherlock Holmes effect" - became much more pronounced. He noticed scuffed shoes, clothing and the occasional black eye. And noticed body language too.

"I was the weird kid, the kid who was off in the corner who didn't fit in," Scott says "I went through a lot of experiences in my life, and I could detect them in other people. I could see stuff that was happening" - a fight, a breakup or a failed test - and confront them about it." Scott drifted from the traditional magic tricks, which he claims never to have liked very much anyway and turned to psychology textbooks.

AND NOW? Scott Xavier performs lectures and entertainments at colleges, fortune 500 companies, universities, festivals, cocktail receptions, charity fundraiser, television, and radio events nation wide!

www.ingramcontent.com/pod-product-compliance
Lightning Source LLC
Chambersburg PA
CBHW031940110426
42744CB00028B/150